V is for Volunteer

A Tennessee Alphabet

Written by Michael Shoulders and Illustrated by Bruce Langton

Sleeping Bear Press
310 North Main Street, Suite 300
Chelsea, MI 48118
www.sleepingbearpress.com

© 2004 Thomson Gale, a part of the Thomson Corporation.

Thomson, Star Logo and Sleeping Bear Press are trademarks
and Gale is a registered trademark used herein under license.

Printed and bound in China.
10 9 8 7 6 5 4

Library of Congress Cataloging-in-Publication Data
Shoulders, Michael
V is for volunteer : a Tennesse alphabet / by Michael Shoulders.
p. cm.
ISBN: 1-58536-033-3
1. Tennessee—Juvenile literature. 2. English language—Alphabet—Juvenile literature.
[1. Tennessee—Miscellanea. 2. Alphabet.] I. Title.
F436.3 .S54 2001
976.8 [E]—dc21
2001020946

For my daughter, Meghann, you mean everything to me, from A to Z.
To Pam Munoz Ryan, one of America's greatest writers of
children's books, I am blessed to call you friend.
Special thanks to Martha Wiley, Brenda Hensley, and Rachel Shepherd.
Finally, to Heather Hughes and Bruce Langton, your patience is
evidence of the enormity of the human heart!

MICHAEL SHOULDERS

For Rebecca, Brett and Rory...without the three of you, my life
would not be complete. You will be in my heart forever.

My thanks to Sleeping Bear Press and Mike Shoulders for all their
hard work in making this book come to life.

BRUCE LANGTON

Come inside—to Tennessee,
    its people, places and history.
Turn the pages—so much to see.
    Start with "A" and end with "Z."

The Appalachian Mountains extend 1,600 miles from central Alabama to Maine. These mountains form the eastern section of Tennessee. The Appalachians abound with plants, animals, and recreational opportunities.

The tulip poplar was chosen as the state tree because it grows all across Tennessee. The pioneers used the poplar hardwood to construct houses, barns, and other farm buildings.

Tennessee's Ocoee River was the site for the 1996 Olympic white water canoe and kayak competition.

A is for Appalachian Mountains
rising tall and grand.
They're home to bear and eagle
and where tulip poplars stand.

Aa

Beale Street extends east from the Mississippi River and is one of Memphis's most famous streets. William Christopher Handy (W.C.), a son of former slaves, was born in Florence, Alabama. He struggled to earn a living playing the cornet in bands across America. At the age of 32, W.C. Handy came to Beale Street. He composed a mayoral campaign song for E.H. Crump. The song, originally named "Mister Crump," was changed to "Memphis Blues" and became a smash hit in Memphis. Later, his "St. Louis Blues" received wider popularity, and W.C. Handy became known as "Father of the Blues."

Today, blues and jazz can be heard in clubs all along Beale Street. Visitors listen to The Blues and dine on traditional Southern foods such as ribs, cornbread, and bar-b-que.

B b

B can stand for Beale Street,
the birthplace of The Blues.
It's where people dance or tap their toes
and dine on bar-b-que.

Clogging is an authentic American dance form, originating in the southern Appalachian Mountains. It is a blend of the Scottish and Irish clog, Native American traditional dance, and African American buck dance. Clogging differs from buck dance in that cloggers usually dance in synchronized steps. Occasionally, individuals come to the front of the group to "do a shine" of improvised dance steps. Clogging steps have interesting names like "rocking chair," "chug," and "buck step."

Today, cloggers dance to many types of music, including rap.

C can be for Cloggers
dancing to a country beat.
They "buck" and "chug" to "Rocky Top"
and quickly move their feet.

Each spring daffodils and dogwood trees bloom to signal the beginning of Tennessee's spring. Daffodils are considered one of the easiest flowers to grow. Their toxic (poisonous) bulbs keep them safe from rodents and insects. Dogwoods have showy spring flowers, red autumn leaves, and red berries that attract birds in winter.

Daffodils and Dogwood Trees
begin with the letter D.
Their blooms tell us it's time for spring,
a one-hundred percent guarantee.

E e

Elvis Presley begins with **E**.
He really loved to sing.
He sang so well that people started
calling him "The King!"

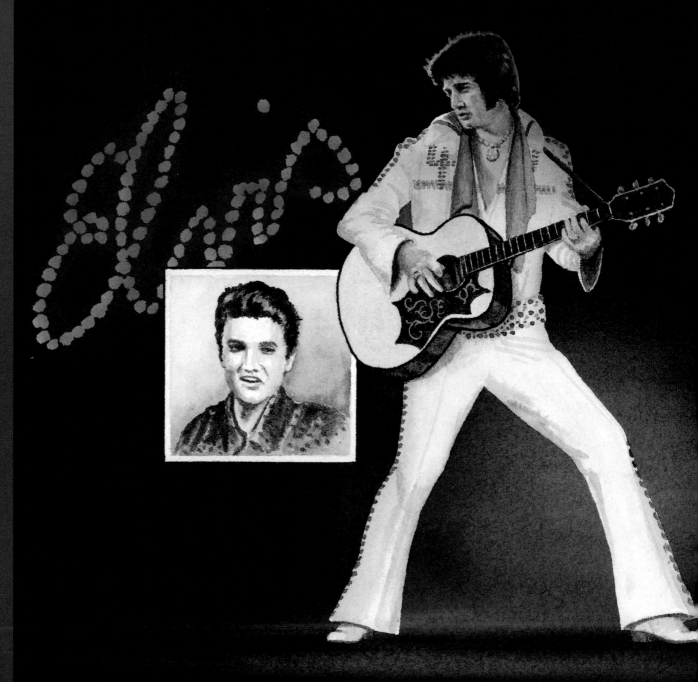

Elvis Presley helped turn rock-n-roll into a musical phenomenon. Elvis made his first record at Sun Records Company in Memphis in 1954. His hits included "Hound Dog," "All Shook Up," and "Love Me Tender."

Elvis's home, Graceland, is located just south of Memphis on Old U.S. Highway 51. Elvis bought Graceland in 1957 at the age of twenty-two. He died there on August 16, 1977. In 1982, Graceland was opened to the public as a house museum with an estimated 650,000 visitors each year. Today, this section of U.S. Highway 51 has been renamed Elvis Presley Boulevard.

Elvis is considered one of the most successful entertainers of the twentieth century.

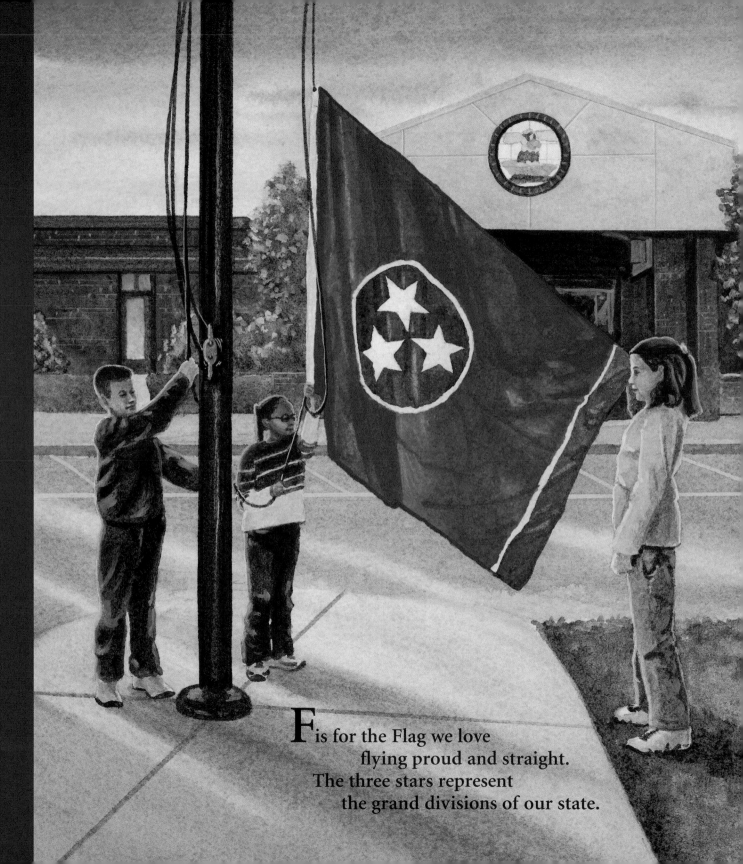

The state flag was designed by LeRoy Reeves. It was approved on April 17, 1905. The three pure white stars represent the three grand divisions of Tennessee: the mountains in the east, the rolling hills of middle Tennessee, and the flat, lush section of the west. The stars are bound together in a circle on a field of blue to show our state's unity. A blue bar along one edge keeps the flag from showing too much red when hanging limp.

Ff

F is for the Flag we love
flying proud and straight.
The three stars represent
the grand divisions of our state.

G is for the Grand Ole Opry,
where country stars appear.
And fans take pictures of favorite singers
to keep as souvenirs.

G is also for Goo Goo Candy Bars. They have sponsored the Grand Ole Opry for years. The Grand Ole Opry announcer says, "Go get a Goo Goo... they're Gooooood!" The Goo Goo Cluster is made of caramel, chocolate, marshmallow, and peanuts. Production of the Goo Goo began in 1912, and it is considered to be the first combination candy bar.

The Grand Ole Opry is the longest continuous running radio show in U.S. history. The first radio broadcast of what would become the Grand Ole Opry took place in October 1925. On November 28 of that same year, the Grand Ole Opry was officially born.

Today, the Opry performances take place in the 4,400-seat Opry House. Many shows are sold out months in advance.

H h

Honeybees begin with H.
They make honey thick and sweet.
Use it with your toast or tea
for a delicious treat.

The honeybee is Tennessee's official state agricultural insect. Honeybees are social insects and are fundamental in the production of all crops. In addition to playing an essential role in pollinating crops, they produce honey and beeswax.

The firefly (lightning bug) and the lady beetle (ladybug) are considered Tennessee's state insects. The firefly has chemicals in its abdomen that produce light. The firefly uses the flashing light to attract a mate. Different species of fireflies can recognize each other by their flashing patterns and rhythms.

The ladybug is considered a living pesticide. Like the tyrannosaurus rex, ladybugs are meat eaters. They love to eat crop pests such as aphids. Farmers buy ladybugs to help control pests.

I is for the Iris.
Some think it's kind of weird:
our state flower has no hair,
but yet it has a beard!

The iris was selected as the state's cultivated flower in 1933. Iris blooms come in several different colors, but the Purple Iris is commonly accepted as the state flower. The fuzzy part of the bloom is called a beard.

I i

The Jubilee Singers were formed in 1871 on the campus of Fisk University in Nashville. Their school, just four years old, was housed in a decaying Union army hospital. To raise funds for repairs, the school's choir toured the United States.

When the Jubilee Singers began their tour, they sang well-known religious songs of the time. However, when they began performing Negro spirituals (often called slave songs) as part of their encore, the crowds demanded more. Soon the group was singing mostly slave songs during their entire performances.

By 1873 the Jubilee Singers were so famous, they traveled to England to perform for Queen Victoria. Although they raised over $50,000 and saved Fisk University, none of the original nine Jubilee Singers ever graduated.

J j

Jubilee Singers begins with J.
They performed so long ago.
Singing African American songs
and of chariots swinging so low.

Knoxville starts with the letter K.
They had a World's Fair there.
People came from around the globe
to learn and play and share.

The Knoxville World's Fair was held from May until October 1982. President Ronald Reagan attended the opening-day ceremonies and welcomed nineteen other nations to the exposition. Over eleven million people visited the fair.

Knoxville is also the headquarters of the Tennessee Valley Authority (TVA). The TVA was formed by Congress in 1933 to help control flooding in the Tennessee Valley, provide cheap electric power, and create water routes for boats. Today, the TVA is the largest public power company in America, providing 8,000,000 people with electricity.

Lookout Mountain extends into parts of Tennessee, Alabama, and Georgia. It is a major tourist destination overlooking Chattanooga, Tennessee that draws thousands of visitors every year. At Lookout Mountain, visitors can take a guided tour of a cave and see Ruby Falls.

At 145 feet, Ruby Falls is America's tallest underground waterfall open to the public. Geological formations in the cave include stalactites, stalagmites, columns, drapes and flowstones. It's easy to remember the differences between stalactites and stalagmites because stalactites hold "tight" to the top of the cave. A column is formed when a stalactite and stalagmite form a single structure. To get a great picture of stalactites, stalagmites and columns, turn to the "X" page!

L is for Lookout Mountain.
Its view is truly great.
On a clear day visitors can see
into parts of seven states.

The state bird is the Mockingbird.
It starts with the letter M.
It mimics the songs of other birds
as it sits upon a limb.

Most birds sing their own songs. But the mockingbird (*Mimus polyglottos*) likes to copy the songs of other birds and the squeals and barks of animals!

Both males and females build a nest where three to six eggs will be laid. The eggs are pale blue-green with brown spots. Mockingbirds eat insects, spiders, berries, and seeds. The mockingbird was chosen the state bird in 1933 after a statewide election.

To attract mockingbirds to your yard, place raisins, sunflower seeds, and slices of oranges and apples on a platform feeder.

m
M

Nashville begins with the letter N.
It's the capital of our state.
Lawmakers meet in the "Music City"
to make Tennessee first-rate.

Four towns have served as Tennessee's capital. Knoxville was picked to be the state's first capital from 1796 until 1812. Kingston served as the capital for a single day in 1807 in order to fulfill a treaty made with the Cherokee Indians. The capital moved to Nashville for five years, then back to Knoxville in 1817. Murfreesboro, the geographic center of the state, was named the capital from 1818-1826. Nashville became the state's permanent capital in 1826.

The opossum is North America's only marsupial, which means the female has a pouch and carries her young like a kangaroo. Baby opossums remain in the pouch for about three months. Then they are carried on their mother's back for another two months. An opossum can be frightened to the point that it goes into involuntary shock and appears to be dead. This is called "playing 'possum."

O is for Opossum.
Tennessee has quite a few.
They have a pink nose and a long pink tail
and a pouch like a kangaroo.

Pp

ANDREW JACKSON

P is for the Presidents
who served our country true,
Andrew Jackson, James K. Polk,
and Andrew Johnson, too.

JAMES K. POLK

ANDREW JOHNSON

Andrew Jackson was the seventh president of the United States (1829-1837). He was nicknamed "Old Hickory," because of his toughness during the War of 1812. Jackson became famous when he defeated the British in New Orleans. His house, called The Hermitage, is located just outside Nashville.

James K. Polk was the nation's eleventh president (1845-1849). He was from Columbia, Tennessee. Polk aided the expansion of the United States to the Pacific Ocean.

Andrew Johnson became president after Abraham Lincoln was assassinated. He was our seventeenth president (1865-1869) and lived in Greeneville, Tennessee.

Quilts were made in nearly every household in Tennessee during the 1800s. Quilt patterns were designed to represent people, events, or the environment. One famous quilt pattern designed by a Tennessean was "Twin Roses." It was in honor of twin girls named Rose and Rosella. The girls lived only a week and their mother wanted a special way to remember them.

New quilt patterns are constantly being created. Recent patterns have names like "Volunteers of Tennessee," "Tennessee Dogwood," "Cumberland Gap," and "Memphis Cotton." Perhaps you can design a quilt to represent your family, town or school!

Q can stand for comfy Quilts,
a pioneer art form.
Stitched by loving hands with friends,
they kept frontiersmen warm.

The raccoon is our state wild animal. They are streaked with gray and have a black face mask. Their tails are marked with five to ten alternating light and dark rings. Usually, two to five young are born to a mother raccoon. Baby raccoons are born without teeth! Their eyes open after two weeks of age. The young stay in the den for about eight weeks. Then they will go out with their mother to help forage for food. Mother raccoons and babies will remain together for about a year at which time the youngsters will take off on their own.

Raccoons are omnivores, which means they eat a variety of food. They will eat fish, frogs, acorns, insects, fruit, earthworms, crayfish, and small mammals. Raccoons can weigh up to 30 pounds when fully grown.

Rr

R is for the Raccoon,
with rings around its tail.
His face makes people wonder
if he ought to be in jail!

S is for Sequoyah
and we should not forget
he used marks called "talking leaves"
to create an alphabet!

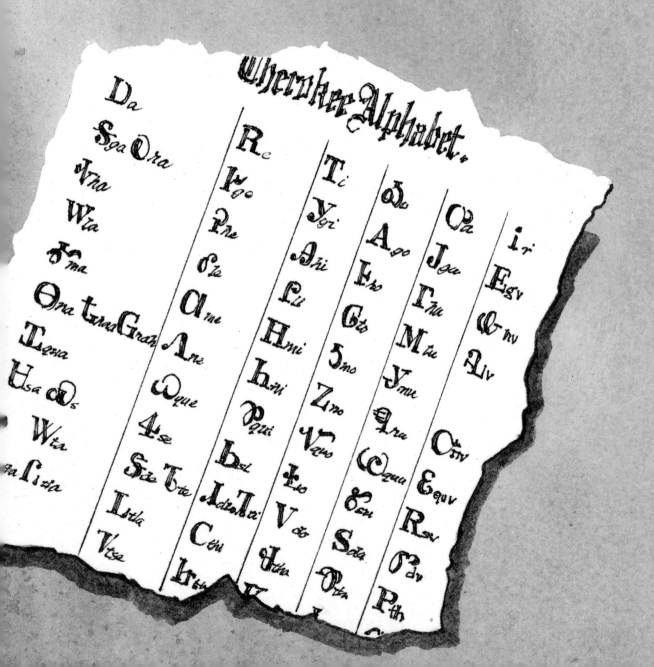

Sequoyah was born in Tennessee and became a talented silversmith. He was fascinated by the European immigrants' ability to communicate with marks on paper. The Cherokee called these marks "talking leaves." Over ten years, Sequoyah isolated eighty-six (later reduced to eighty-five) syllables used in the Cherokee language. He assigned a written symbol for each syllable and the Cherokee alphabet was designed. By 1826 thousands of Cherokee were literate, far surpassing the literacy rate of their European neighbors.

On February 21, 1828, the first Native American newspaper, the *Cherokee Phoenix*, was printed in Cherokee and English.

Ss

Besides slavery, The Trail of Tears is considered the saddest part of Tennessee's history. From May 1838 to March 1839, the federal government removed 16,000 Cherokee from Tennessee, Alabama, Georgia, and North Carolina. Although some Cherokee traveled on boats and in wagons, many walked barefoot the entire way from southeast Tennessee to Oklahoma. Some of the worst droughts and storms in Tennessee's history made the Cherokee's travels difficult. It is believed that over 4,000 Cherokee died on the Trail of Tears.

The Trail of Tears begins with T.
It traveled through Tennessee.
4,000 died when the government removed the native Cherokee.

CHEROKEE

U can be for Unikite
a gem that is unique.
It's often found in the Unaka Mountains
along roads or in mountain creeks.

The Unikite is a gem found in eastern Tennessee. This granite made of pink feldspar and green epidote, is named for the Unaka Mountain range between Tennessee and North Carolina. "Unaka" is taken from the Cherokee word, "Unica," which means white. Unikite is found mostly in the southern United States, but it can also be found in Zimbabwe, Africa. It is said to be a billion years old.

Another gem found in Tennessee is the pearl. The pearl is the state gem and is considered one of the most durable in the world.

U u

V is for Volunteer.
    It's important for you to know
when help is needed anywhere,
        Tennesseans are sure to go.

On May 26, 1847, Governor Brown called for 2,800 Tennesseans to volunteer to fight in the Mexican War. Over 30,000 reported for duty. Since that time, Tennessee has been called "The Volunteer State."

Davy Crockett (1786-1836) is considered one of Tennessee's best-known volunteers and frontier heroes. Crockett was a Tennessee legislator and congressman. When he lost a congressional race in 1835, he volunteered to join Colonel William B. Travis at the Alamo in San Antonio, Texas. On February 22, 1836, Davy Crockett led a group of fifteen Tennessee volunteers to fight at the Alamo. Crockett died at the Alamo in March 1836.

Wilma Rudolph was born in Clarksville, Tennessee. One of twenty-two brothers and sisters, she contracted polio at a young age, and doctors said she'd never walk again. For five years she wore a leg brace and worked to strengthen her legs. Wilma never quit believing in herself. Finally, one day, Wilma walked without her brace. Soon she was playing sports.

When Wilma was fourteen, Edward Temple, a women's track coach, saw her playing basketball and invited her to attend his summer track camp. A year later she earned a place on the U.S. Olympic track team. For four years she trained as a Tennessee Tigerbelle at Tennessee State University. In 1960, in Rome, Wilma became the first woman to win three gold medals in the history of the Olympic Games.

Wilma Rudolph begins with W.
Her story must be told.
She overcame childhood polio
to win Olympic medals of gold.

1940

Xanadu Cave is among the one-hundred largest caves in the world. Located in Fentress County, it is home to insects, crayfish, bats, rats, and even cave fish. The cave fish is a true troglodyte which means that it spends its entire life in complete darkness. Cave fish in Xanadu have no eyes or skin color.

Members of the National Speleological Society or cavers affiliated with a National Speleological Society grotto are the only visitors allowed in Xanadu.

X

X can be for Xanadu Cave,
a dark place, we all agree.
The cave fish there do not have eyes
because they don't need to see!

Yy

Yes, Y is for a Yodel.
Some think it's hard to do.
But all you really have to sing
is "yo-de-lay-hee-hooo!"

"yo-de-lay-hee-hoooo!"

There are several types of yodeling, including Swiss, Alpine, and Country. Country stars who have yodeled on their recordings include Roy Rogers, Gene Autry, and LeAnn Rimes. If you can yell like Tarzan, then you can yodel too!

In the summer of 1994, a biology teacher at Gallatin High School realized Tennessee had never designated a state butterfly. She asked a state legislator if it were possible to make a law naming one. In 1994, the Gallatin High School biology class surveyed every student in Sumner County. Many suggestions were made, but the Zebra Swallowtail (*Eurytides marcellus*) was selected because it is native to our state. Additionally, the only larval host for the Zebra Swallowtail is the paw paw plant, a traditional southern tree. The Zebra Swallowtail has black and white stripes that run the length of its body, and red and blue spots on its lower back. It is found throughout most of the United States.

In 1995, the Zebra Swallowtail became Tennessee's official state butterfly.

Zz

The lovely Zebra Swallowtail begins with the letter Z.
Now stop and think of all you've learned about our Tennessee!

A Mountain of Facts

1. Who is considered "The Father of the Blues"?

2. What do the three stars on the Tennessee state flag represent?

3. What animal is North America's only marsupial?

4. How many medals did Wilma Rudolph win in the 1960 Olympics?

5. What is the name of the cave in Tennessee that has fish with no eyes or skin color?

6. Where did Elvis Presley make his first record?

7. How many seats are in the Opry House?

8. Tennessee has the largest public power company in America. What is it called?

9. There is a section of Rock City where you can see seven states all at once. What are the seven states?

10. What insect helps farmers by eating crop pests?

11. Who had the nickname, "Old Hickory"?

12. The Jubilee Singers toured the United States to raise money for what institution?

13. Approximately how many Cherokee died on The Trail of Tears?

14. Who created the Cherokee alphabet?

15. What gem is said to be a billion years old?

Answers

1. William Christopher Handy.

2. The three white stars represent the three grand divisions of Tennessee: the mountains of east Tennessee, the rolling hills of middle Tennessee, and the flat, lush section of the west.

3. The opossum.

4. Three.

5. Xanadu Cave.

6. Sun Records Company in Memphis.

7. 4,400 seats.

8. Tennessee Valley Authority.

9. Alabama, Georgia, South Carolina, North Carolina, Virginia, Kentucky, and Tennessee.

10. Ladybugs.

11. Andrew Jackson.

12. Fisk University.

13. Over 4,000.

14. Sequoyah.

15. Unikite.

Michael Shoulders

Michael Shoulders is a Title I Supervisor and has worked for the Clarksville-Montgomery County School System for twenty-five years. His "Story Time" column appears every week in the *Clarksville-Leaf Chronicle*. Michael enjoys traveling across Tennessee speaking to educators and children about writing and books. He and his wife, Debbie, share a home with their three children, Jason, Ryan, and Meghann, and standard poodle, Hershey.

Bruce Langton

Bruce Langton is considered a premier contemporary artist. His unmistakable style and unique ability to capture sporting and wildlife scenes as well as contemporary landscapes has won him numerous national awards and international recognition.

With over one hundred limited edition prints and etchings on the market, Bruce is now proud to add children's books to his list of achievements: *B is for Buckeye: An Ohio Alphabet* (his first), *Cardinal Numbers: An Ohio Counting Book, H is for Hoosier: An Indiana Alphabet* and *V is for Volunteer: A Tennessee Alphabet.*

Bruce enjoys illustrating children's books, teaming with his son for professional clown performances, and teaching children Kyokushinkai karate. Bruce resides in Indiana with his wife Rebecca and two sons, Brett and Rory.